Teaching Outstanding Persuasive Writing

by Alan Peat

CREATIVE EDUCATIONAL PRESS LTD

PUBLISHED BY: Creative Educational Press Ltd
                  2 The Walled Garden
                  Grange Park Drive
                  Biddulph
                  Staffs
                  ST8 7TA

                  Tel: 07789938923
                  Fax: 01782 379398

PRINTED BY: York Publishing Services Ltd.,
                  64, Hallfield Road, Layerthorpe, York, YO31 7ZQ

DESIGN: Simon Matthews

PROOFREADING: Angela Burt

Alan Peat   www.alanpeat.com

                  info@alanpeat.com

Simon Matthews   www.s2air.co.uk

                  info@s2air.co.uk

ISBN: 978-0-9544755-1-2

Also available from Creative Educational Press Ltd (www.thecepress.com):

Writing Exciting Sentences: Age 7 Plus by Alan Peat
A Second Book of Exciting Sentences by Alan Peat & Mathew Sullivan
50 Ways to Retell a Story: Cinderella by Alan Peat, Julie Peat and Christopher Storey
Get Your Head Around Punctuation (...and how to teach it!) by Alan Peat
The Elves and The Shoemaker 1897 illustrated by John Harrold
Writing Exciting Ghost Stories: Age 9 Plus: Ghost Story Plot Skeletons by Alan Peat (co-author Julie Barnfather)
Teaching Poetry with 4-8 year olds (Imaginative Minds Publishing)
Teaching Poetry with 7-12 year olds (Imaginative Minds Publishing)
Word Games at Key Stage 2 (Nash Pollock Publishing)
Improving Story Writing KS 1 &2 (Nash Pollock Publishing)
Improving Non-Fiction Writing KS 1 & 2 (co-written with Margaret McNeil) (Nash Pollock Publishing)

CONTENTS

INTRODUCTION

'Teaching Outstanding Persuasive Writing' gives classroom practitioners tried-and-tested teaching strategies which relate to a broad range of key elements of persuasive writing. In the book I consider structural models and easily accessible ideas for developing an embedded understanding of the essential writing features of persuasive texts.

I have divided this book into key themes which help the teacher to plan sharply focused 'persuasive writing' lessons. It will also assist in the process of personalised target setting.

It is my hope, however, that busy teachers will not isolate any of the strategies included as stand-alone lessons. I would rather that they integrate the ideas into exciting writing sessions which relate to both pupils' interests and the broader curriculum.

For ease-of-access the teaching strategies are organised under four key themes:

1. Structural Models
2. Opening Strategies
3. Language Techniques/Features
4. Closing Strategies

The book includes six photocopiable appendices:

1. Sentence starters which support the persuasive viewpoint.
2. Sentence starters which demolish the opposing viewpoint.
3. Sentence starters which conclude the persuasive essay.
4. Persuasive question stems.
5. More powerful words than 'bad'.
6. More powerful words than 'good'.

These should be shared with pupils as a form of language-support. I sincerely hope that this book will enrich both teachers' and pupils' understanding of this engaging genre.

Alan Peat
2011

STRUCTURAL
MODELS

UNDERLYING PRINCIPLES

Before we consider structural models for persuasive essays, a first principle needs to be established. The structural model for any persuasive essay should be simple and straight-forward. If it is complex then the persuasive point will be hard to follow. The teacher needs to keep in mind that persuasive writing has two essential elements:

1. Clear message content.
2. Adept use of persuasive language techniques.

The latter will be dealt with later in this book but at the outset it needs to be understood that 'clear message content' and 'structural simplicity' are closely interlocked. Structural complexity hinders, rather than assists, in the process of 'reader yielding'. 'Reader yielding' occurs when the reader has been persuaded to agree with the viewpoint of the essay's author – the whole point of a persuasive piece of writing!

Although no text form can be reduced to a structural formula, there are clear models which work well with seven to sixteen-year-olds. Before exploring these we need to consider a question:

What is the first stage in planning a persuasive essay?

The answer, once again, is simple. The first stage should always be to define the outcome. Before focusing on any structural model I always ask pupils to complete the following sentence:

At the end of my persuasive essay the reader will agree that _____ .

Once the outcome has been agreed, then I ask the pupils to 'keep this in mind' during the writing process. The rationale which underpins this approach is obvious; if you know what you are aiming at then you stand some chance of hitting the target.

I have also included in this book a verbal reminder for writers of ALL pieces of persuasive text and a simple visual layout which can be adapted to include any combination of structural model, opening strategies, language techniques/features and closing strategies. This is based on a diamond shape, and the catchphrase "Make your point ... Expand your point ..... Make your point again!"

MAKE YOUR POINT!

EXPAND
YOUR POINT

MAKE YOUR POINT AGAIN!

THE THREE KEY STRUCTURAL MODELS

When working on persuasive writing with a class/group of pupils I use the following three structural models. I teach all three so that the pupils have a structural 'menu of possibilities' from which to select. It should be remembered that some of the best writers break all the rules and as long as the desired outcome ('Reader yielding') is achieved, all variants on these three models are perfectly acceptable.

The three structural models are;

1. The 'Courtroom' model.

2. The 'Problem/Solution' model.

3. The 'Aristotelian' model.

STRUCTURAL MODEL ONE
THE 'COURTROOM' MODEL

This simple, three-point model can be incredibly powerful. The worst outcome of any persuasive essay is confusion. This model, often used by lawyers when presenting cases, limits the structural potential for confusion.

Model

i. STATE
State position (good/bad).

ii. BACK-UP
Give back-up evidence for your position.

iii. RESTATE
Restate your position.

The repetition, inherent in this model, makes key points memorable.

This structural model can be represented using the diamond shape as below:

MAKE YOUR POINT!

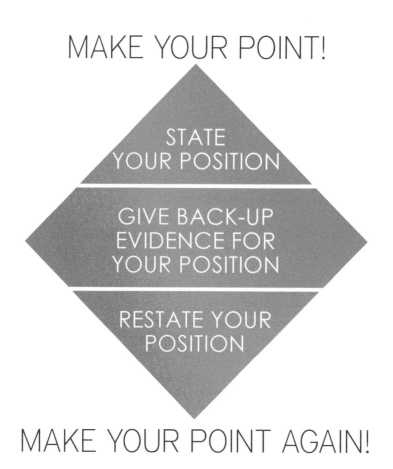

STATE
YOUR POSITION

GIVE BACK-UP
EVIDENCE FOR
YOUR POSITION

RESTATE YOUR
POSITION

MAKE YOUR POINT AGAIN!

STRUCTURAL MODEL TWO
THE PROBLEM/SOLUTION MODEL

i. PROBLEM
State what the problem is.

ii. ADDRESS
Explain the range of ways in which the problem could be addressed, giving details and examples.

iii. SOLUTION
State how the problem will be solved (if the points made in ii are followed).

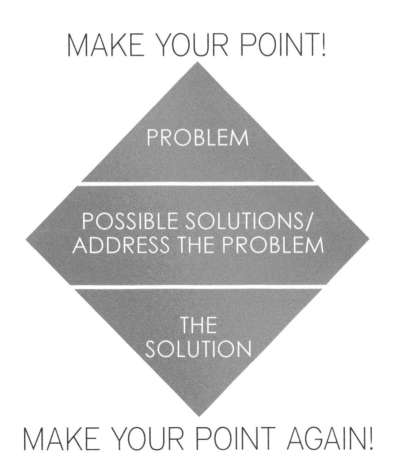

MAKE YOUR POINT!

PROBLEM

POSSIBLE SOLUTIONS/
ADDRESS THE PROBLEM

THE
SOLUTION

MAKE YOUR POINT AGAIN!

STRUCTURAL MODEL THREE
THE ARISTOTELIAN MODEL

i. WHAT I THINK
Overview of essay (this can be a statement of the author's position).

ii. WHY I THINK IT
Range of arguments which support persuasive point of essay.

iii. WHAT OTHERS THINK
Acknowledgement of alternative viewpoints (with refutations included).

iv. WHY I STILL THINK IT
Summary and 'call to action' (what you want the reader to do now!).

MAKE YOUR POINT!

WHAT I THINK

WHY I THINK IT

WHAT OTHERS THINK

WHY I STILL THINK IT

MAKE YOUR POINT AGAIN!

This four-point model is actually a simplified version of the original six-point Aristotelian model. For the sake of consistency the original comprised:

i. Exordium – overview.

ii. Narratio – current position.

iii. Diviso – a break-down of areas to be discussed.

iv. Confirmatio – arguments supporting the position.

v. Confutatio – Refutation of counter position.

vi. Conclusio – Mix of emotional or logical 'call to action'.

USING THE STRUCTURAL MODELS

The rest of this book consists of effective openings, writing techniques and closing strategies, which the persuasive writer can employ to create a piece of writing which does the job – persuades the reader! To return to a point I made on page 2: "The structural model for any persuasive essay should be simple and straightforward."

Within each of these structural models, however, the language and techniques used can be complex and varied. On page 60 I have provided an example of an Aristotelian model laid out in the diamond shape, with some suggestions/tips for techniques the writer could include.

OPENING STRATEGIES

At the start of all great speeches, there is an attention-grabber, a 'hook' which grabs the attention of the audience, captivates them and holds them.

Effective persuasive essays are no different, it's just that the 'hook' is written rather than spoken. Able (...or more fortunate) pupils learn these 'hooks' by reading widely. There are, however, many which can be modelled and explicitly discussed in class, thereby speeding up the process of assimilation, then application. Examples of a range of effective, easy-to-teach persuasive essay openers are detailed in this chapter.

All of the opening strategies listed in this chapter can be adapted and used within ANY of the structural models defined in the previous chapter.

OPENER ONE

Short story with bad ending + (a '...could...if')
sentence + what you are arguing against =
a great opener!

Example:
*John was a friendly, well-liked, loving boy. He was loved by his mum, dad, gran and grandad. He
was also loved by all his classmates. One day John forgot to look left and right when he came to the
busy road in front of his school. Instead he stepped onto the road and a speeding car hit him. John
was killed by that speeding car and every day since he has been missed by everyone who knew him.*

This is exactly what could happen if the road is built in front of our primary school.

Overview

The persuasive opening example given above is based on a hypothetical premise with a possible
consequence: "If a road is built a child could be killed". This possible consequence is then turned into
a short vignette. It is, in a sense, a 'Flashforward' and, although complex to explain, many pupils do
grasp the form through the deconstruction of modelled examples.

How much more powerful is:
*"John was a friendly, well-liked, loving boy. He was loved by his mum, dad, gran and grandad. He was
also loved by all his classmates. One day John forgot to look left and right when he came to the busy
road in front of his school. Instead he stepped onto the road and a speeding car hit him. John was
killed by that speeding car and every day since he has been missed by everyone who knew him.
This is exactly what could happen if the road is built in front of our primary school."*

Than:
"If a road is built a child could be killed".

Key teaching points

1. Open the persuasive text with a story about something terrible that might happen in the
   future if the 'thing', which the rest of the persuasive text is arguing against, happens. In this
   instance the construction of a road which is proposed in front of a Primary School.

2. Follow this story with a '...could...if' sentence, the purpose of which is to demonstrate that the
   terrible event hasn't actually occurred but it could if the thing being argued against occurs.

3. Stress the need to use a real name, rather than writing 'a boy' or 'a girl'. This personalises
   the text.

4. Draw attention to the repetition of the name 'John' throughout the story. The effect of this is
   an increased chance of empathic concern from the reader.

OPENER TWO

Short story + 'This will all change if .....' sentence + what you are arguing against = a great opener!

Example:
John is a carefree boy. He sometimes runs all the way to school without stopping even once! He doesn't have to worry about cars racing by; he doesn't have to worry about speeding lorries; he doesn't have to worry about huge, heavy trucks. This is because John doesn't have to worry about crossing a busy road on his way to school.

This will all change if the proposed road, directly in front of our school, is built. In this essay I will explain exactly why John should remain carefree and exactly why the road MUST NOT be constructed.

Overview

The above example is similar to Opener One, though the first paragraph of Opener Two paints an idyllic picture of the current situation rather than a negative picture of a possible future consequence.

The idyllic first paragraph is shattered by the sentence which opens the second paragraph: 'This will all change if ...'. This categorical statement maintains that the current situation will alter for the worse if the 'thing' (which the rest of the persuasive essay will argue against) happens.

Key teaching points

1. As with Opener One, real names rather than personal pronouns should be used. The name should be repeated in order to increase the chance of an empathic response from the reader.

2. Lists should be used. In the above example, a statement list (each statement separated from the next with a semicolon) is used to show that John doesn't have to worry about three things:
    - cars racing by
    - speeding lorries
    - huge, heavy trucks.
    The implication being that, if the road is built, John will not just have to worry about one danger, he will have all three to worry about. The list amplifies the emotive appeal.

3. Note also that the choice of adjectives– "speeding", "racing" serve to heighten the sense of implied danger. This should be discussed with pupils.

4. Perhaps most importantly, the risks John will have to worry about if the road is built grow worse as the list lengthens; speeding lorries are greater risks than cars racing by, and huge heavy trucks are even worse! The building of tension adds drama to the piece of persuasive writing. This language technique is NOT limited to persuasive writing openers and is discussed further on page 26.

OPENER THREE
'Them' and 'us' opening

Example:
Some people don't want to think about the new road. Some people think that, if they don't mention the new road, it will go away. Some people just ignore the idea of the new road.

We, however, do want to mention the new road. We do want to talk about it. We know that if we do nothing then the new road will be built and that would be disastrous.

Overview

In this opening technique, 'them' and 'us' provides an opportunity for polarising the positions in an argument. The point of a persuasive essay is, of course, to persuade the reader to agree with a certain point of view, to join 'us' against 'them'.

The 'We...' sentences demonstrate that the consequences of inaction will be disastrous.
Once again, this is a difficult essay opening to explain without the use of a modelled example.

Key teaching points

1.   The use of the inclusive 'we' allies the reader with the author of the persuasive text.

2.   The repeating list of sentences which open with 'Some people ...' indicates that there is one group of people (others) who want to take no action while 'we' are in the right, and want to take action to stop the road being built.

OPENER FOUR
'Expert friend' talking to reader

Example:
I've been a doctor now for more than 30 years and I've seen these changes at first hand.

I know that you know that obesity will, very soon, be one of the U.K.'s biggest killers.

The question is, how can we persuade others that obesity needs to be tackled? And how can we persuade them that the issue is an urgent one?

Overview

To produce this opener, an 'expert' must address the reader and introduce the issue/concern.

Obviously the 'expert' must be chosen from the appropriate field of expertise needed to comment on the issue at hand: doctors for a medical problem, professors for an academic discussion, solicitors for a legal point etc. Following this, the opening should always end with a direct appeal to the reader to help the expert to address the issue. This often takes the form of repeated questions.

Key teaching points

1. The opening should always be in the first person and the writer should adopt the frame of reference of the expert (doctor, professor, lawyer, teacher etc.).

2. The credibility of the expert should be established. In the given example '30 years' of service adds credibility.

3. As in Opener Three, the use of the inclusive word 'we' seeks to ally the reader with the sensible point of view of the respected 'expert'.

4. The repeated questioning technique also reinforces this feeling of inclusion, implying a 'team spirit' approach to tackling the problem, and these questions also grow in importance, first "the issue needs to be tackled", then "the issue is an urgent one".

OPENER FIVE

Worried about ....? There's no need! However .....

Example:

Worried about the mere problem of (getting wrinkles)? *There's no need!*

However, you do need to worry about (the effect fatty food is having on your vital internal organs) ...

Overview

This opening strategy begins with a well-known emotional insecurity, then persuades the insecure reader that there are more important issues to consider.

The technique of confronting an unfounded fear is useful in any persuasive essay. It demonstrates that, while trivial issues may cause concern, more serious issues should really be foremost in the reader's mind. It also adds a personalised dimension.

Key teaching points

1.   When teaching this persuasive essay opening, draw attention to the punctuation in the opening line (question mark, then exclamation mark). Pupils are then less likely to leave them out.

2.   The word 'mere' is very important. It adds weight to the persuasive point that 'looks' are unimportant. Pupils may be asked to use a thesaurus and collect synonyms for the word 'mere'.

3.   The introduction of the line "However, you do need to worry about ..." then allows the author to move on and introduce the key point of the persuasive essay.

OPENER SIX

Worried about X? You should be!

Example:
Worried about Bird Flu? You should be! In this essay I'll persuade you why Bird Flu is one of the biggest threats which humanity has ever faced.

Overview

This opening strategy is the opposite of Opener Five: it affirms a fear which is totally founded. The following essay then consists of reasons and details which support the initial fear.

Key teaching points

1.   When teaching this persuasive essay opening, as in Opener Five, draw attention to the punctuation in the opening line (question mark, then exclamation mark).

2.   The second line "In this essay ..." gives the author an ideal opportunity at which he/she can "Make the point" of the essay (see page 3).

OPENER SEVEN

Opposite/Ridiculous

Example:
Doing no exercise at all is a fantastic idea!

Clearly, this is ridiculous and I'll now prove why it is so ridiculous.

Overview

This opening has three separated elements -

1.   A statement of the direct opposite of your persuasive point.

2.   A following sentence which explicitly states that the statement is ridiculous/ludicrous etc.

3.   A series of reasons and examples which support the persuasive point (in this instance, the necessity of exercise).

Key teaching points

1.   When teaching this, I ban the words 'good' and 'bad' and replace them with alternatives like 'fantastic' and 'ridiculous'. We then hunt for further synonyms for these words.*

2.   The structure of this opening gives another excellent way for the writer to "Make their point".

* A useful website for this is: www.visualthesaurus.com

OPENER EIGHT

Do not x 4. Do x 1.

Example:
In our school we do not accept violence; we do not tolerate bullying; we do not accept intolerance; we do not allow fighting. In our school we do something different - we all work happily together.

In this essay I will persuade you that our school's approach would work well in your school too.

Overview

This opening relies on the rhetorical technique of anaphora, where a phrase is repeated at the beginning of successive sentences or clauses. It is inspired by Winston Churchill's speeches, for example:

"We shall not flag or fail. We shall fight in France; we shall fight on the seas and the oceans; we shall fight with growing confidence .... ".

Key teaching points

1. Focus on the use of semicolons in the statement list or pupils will incorrectly revert to commas.

2. Over-use of anaphora will limit the impact. Establish an upper limit of 4 phrases in the list.

OPENER NINE

They say x 3. We say x1.

Overview

Another use of a Churchillian strategy (see Opener Eight) except that in this example the technique is to posit, then deflate the opposing argument.

Key teaching points

1. Note the use of 'they' and 'we', which is similar to the 'Them and Us' position in Opener Three. Again, the technique encourages the taking of sides. Hopefully we can persuade the reader to be part of 'our' team.

2. The use of deliberately repetitive sentence starters underpins this 'them' and 'us' position and adds drama to the writing.

3. A thesaurus could be used to find words other than 'convince' which could be used in this, or other persuasive essays.

4. Again, set a ceiling on the "They say" statements or the impact of the technique will be diminished. Add a number to the title, as I have, to avoid this problem.

OPENER TEN
Multisensory Appeal

In order to demonstrate the efficacy of this approach I have included a weak opening <u>without</u> multisensory appeal, followed by an altered version with multisensory appeal.

Examples

A. Without Multisensory Appeal

Why don't we want a road near our school? That's not difficult to answer: because children could be killed.

B. Improved by including Multisensory Appeal

Why don't we want a road near our school? That's not difficult to answer. When a car impacts with a child hard metal thuds into soft flesh. You can smell the burning rubber of the tyres. There is a sudden, sickening thud. Do you want me to go on?

Overview

Often words stimulate our visual imagination but in some of the most powerful, evocative cases, words are used to appeal to a range of our senses. 'Multisensory appeal' is a key element of effective persuasive writing and should not just be confined to essay openings.

Key teaching points

1.   Use the two examples given above as a stimulus for discussion. Focus on the question, 'Why is B. more effective?'

2.   Encourage pupils to find words and phrases which appeal to different senses. 'Hard metal thuds into soft flesh' – appeals to the sense of touch. It creates a tactile image.

        'You can smell burning rubber' provides an olfactory appeal, while 'sudden sickening thud' is an auditory appeal.

OPENER ELEVEN
'Yoked opener' x2 sentences/phrases

Example:
Building a road in front of our school will be incredibly dangerous.
Dangerous for parents, teachers and children.

Overview

This opening, like Opener Eight, relies on repetition, in this case the repetition of the last word of the previous sentence at the start of the following sentence. As long as the words are chosen carefully, it can be a dramatic and effective introduction to a persuasive text. This technique can also be used to great effect in narrative writing and should not be limited to the opening of a piece of persuasive writing. It is discussed further on page 27.

Key teaching points

1.	Children need to think carefully about the words they want to use at the end of one sentence and the start of the next. Allow planning time and redrafting to produce the most effective combination of words.

2.	Apply a maximum limit of two yoked sentences in each example to avoid a contrived 'feel'.

The final two openers are self-explanatory and so only examples are included.

OPENER TWELVE

Question which includes one viewpoint and the opposing viewpoint

Example
Is it more acceptable for teachers to choose what pupils eat or for pupils to choose for themselves?

OPENER THIRTEEN

Negative - positive questions
OR
Positive - Negative questions

Example
A. Do you want to die young or do you want to live a long and healthy life?
OR
B. Do you want healthy food which will give you plenty of energy or unhealthy food that will make you feel sleepy?

LANGUAGE
TECHNIQUES/FEATURES

The following, directly teachable, language techniques/features are dealt with in no particular order and need not be taught in any particular order.

They have all, however, been successful for me in the classroom and should be taught as and when the teacher decides it is cognitively appropriate.

Put simply, the greater the range of aptly applied language features, the more persuasive the argument is likely to be.

Effective persuasive essays combine two elements:

1. Clear message content.
2. Creative delivery of that message.

The use of a broad spectrum of language techniques enhances both of these key elements.

LANGUAGE TECHNIQUE ONE
F.A.C.T. S.T.O.R.E.

'Fact Store' is an exceedingly useful acronym which helps pupils to remember the broad range of forms of supporting evidence which they should use to reinforce their persuasive point.

The meaning is explained below:

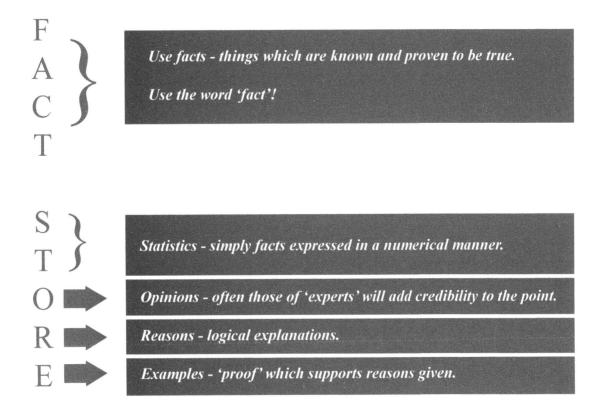

F
A
C
T
> *Use facts - things which are known and proven to be true.*
>
> *Use the word 'fact'!*

S
T
> *Statistics - simply facts expressed in a numerical manner.*

O → *Opinions - often those of 'experts' will add credibility to the point.*

R → *Reasons - logical explanations.*

E → *Examples - 'proof' which supports reasons given.*

I simply display and discuss the acronym and, prior to writing a persuasive piece, I remind the children to check that they've included all of the elements of 'Fact Store'.

LANGUAGE TECHNIQUE TWO

It gets worse/better! sentences (Dramatic heightening)

These are best explained by example:

Examples

> 1. *Would you ignore something which could <u>harm</u>, <u>disfigure</u> or even <u>kill</u> a child?*

NOTE: 'harm' is the first emotive word to be used in the sentence. It is followed by 'disfigure' which is more serious than the word 'harm' and finally the word 'kill': the most serious possible outcome in this situation. This dramatic heightening technique adds weight to the point and delivers a 'persuasive punch' at the end of the sentence.

Two further examples are included below. Note that in example 3, this has been inverted to promote the more positive aspect of an argument.

> 2. *If the road is built motorbikes will <u>pass</u> close by, cars will <u>speed</u> past and lorries will <u>hurtle</u> along.*

> 3. *If you help one person, it will make you <u>smile</u>; if you help someone else it will make you <u>happy</u> all day; if you help a third person you'll feel <u>great for the whole week</u>.*

LANGUAGE TECHNIQUE THREE
Yoked Sentences

In yoked sentences the last word of the previous sentence becomes the first word of the following sentence. Controlled repetition is a significant tool to be used in both spoken and written persuasion.

It should be stressed that the word to be repeated should be carefully chosen – usually it will have significant emotive impact. If the word to be repeated is not chosen carefully, the technique becomes redundant.

Note that if the 'Yoked Opener x 2' (Opener Eleven on page 21) has been used, children should be discouraged from using this in the main body of the piece of persuasive writing or the power of the techniques becomes diluted and the writing can appear stilted.

Examples

Good Example: *Building a motorway near our school would be <u>disastrous</u>! <u>Disastrous</u> because children will certainly be at risk.*

Bad Example: *A motorway should not be built near our <u>school</u>. <u>School</u> would be better off without it.*

LANGUAGE TECHNIQUE FOUR
Do we want...? No!/Yes!

These should not be overused or the technique will seem contrived. If necessary create a ceiling of no more than one (or two) in any essay.

The rhetorical question should be followed by a simple, short, absolute answer. An exclamation mark can add emphasis to this answer and pupils' attention should be drawn to the correct use of both the first question mark and subsequent exclaimed answer.

Examples

> *Do we want a road near our school? Of course we don't!*
> *Do we want unhealthy, fatty food served to us at lunchtime? Of course not!*
> OR
> *Do we want our children to walk to school in safety? Of course, we do!*
> *Do we want healthy, tasty food that will do us good for lunch? Yes, we do!*

NOTE: The dramatic effect of this technique can be doubled by alternating the positive /negative questions in two consecutive sentences in the main body of the persuasive writing.

> *Do we want unhealthy, fatty food served to us at lunchtime? Of course not! Do we want healthy, tasty food that will do us good for lunch? Yes, we do!*

LANGUAGE TECHNIQUE FIVE
'How would you feel if ....?'

Aristotle divided persuasion into three categories: pathos, logos and ethos.

Pathos – appealing to the audience's (reader's or listener's) emotions is a key and very powerful aspect of the persuasive essay. The personal appeal to "you" or "your/s" is a direct appeal to the reader's emotional core.

Use any question which begins with the stem 'How would you feel if ....?

Example

> *How would you feel if your child attended a school which didn't promote healthy eating?*
>
> *Would you allow that?*

The example above doubles the emotional appeal through the inclusion of a second question with a 'Would you ....?' stem.

Logos - persuasion by demonstration of proof, real or apparent.

Example

> *Schools which do not promote healthy eating are seriously harming the health of hundreds of pupils. How would you feel if your child attended such a school?*

Ethos - an appeal from someone with a vested interest in the matter.

Example

> *I would be extremely unhappy if my child attended a school which did not promote healthy eating. Wouldn't you?*

LANGUAGE TECHNIQUE SIX
Named example

This is a powerful tool in the persuasive toolkit.

When we illustrate a persuasive point with a named example, we move from the generic to the specific. It also provides us with a narrative-within-the-persuasive-text. Note also the use of a percentage, which adds factual validity to the argument (see next page).

Example

Main roads should not be built near schools. One example, which clearly demonstrates why they shouldn't, is St. Monkton's Primary School. When a main road was built nearby, traffic-related incidents increased by 21% in less than two years.

LANGUAGE TECHNIQUE SEVEN
Using Statistics

Statistics provide the reader with quantitative data which supports the persuasive point. They can take several forms:

1. Simple numeric

Example: *After the road was built, five pupils said they couldn't hear as well in class.*

2. Percentages

Example: *In the year since the road was built there has been a 12.8% increase in chest infections.*

3. Pie charts

Easy to understand, the pie chart shows how the whole of something is divided. Each segment should be a different colour so that visual clarity is maximised.

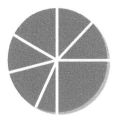

4. Graphs

A useful way of visually representing data, line graphs are a much-used aspect of persuasive texts.

5. Bar charts

These are fantastic for 'before and after' data representations. Note: bars can be either vertical or horizontal.

Key Teaching Point

You will need to decide on a 'house style' for statistics, numerals etc. If a pupil writes out "fifteen per cent" in one sentence, then uses "15%" in another, then the lack of consistency will weaken the strength of the writing.
As a rule:

A.   Write percentages as: 15%, 8% etc.
B.   For numbers up to ten, write them out, e.g. one, five, nine, ten etc. Above ten, use numerals: 33, 44, 17 etc.

LANGUAGE TECHNIQUE EIGHT
I do not want to (x3) ... I only want to (x1)

Example

> *I do not want to[1] stop you from having fun. I do not want to[2] stop you from enjoying yourself. I do not want to[3] spoil your weekends. I only want to[1] ask you to think before you drink.*

The thrice repeated, 'I do not want to' sentences emphasise a broad range of the positive things that the persuader/writer doesn't want to end. These are then followed with the 'persuasive punch line' which emphasises the key persuasive point of the essay, the thing the writer does want to stop.

This technique can be useful within a persuasive text. It can also be used effectively at either the opening or end of the writing. However, if it is used within the text, avoid using it at the start or end as well, or vice versa.

LANGUAGE TECHNIQUE NINE
Expert witness

The provision of an 'expert witness' is a key element of court cases. It is equally useful in a persuasive essay, as the 'expert' lends credence, validity and 'weight' to the persuasive point. Useful experts to invoke include,

A.   Professors
B.   Doctors
C.   Lawyers
D.   Pathologists

Sometimes the expert isn't specified – the mere reference to experts as "many experts agree" can still act as a 'persuasive support'.

Statistics, percentages, graphs and pie charts also sit well with 'expert' evidence.

LANGUAGE TECHNIQUE TEN
Time Running Out

A sense of urgency can be a useful way of heightening the impact of the essay, concluding with a 'Call to Action'.

I often display 'Time running out _____.' phrases and sentences when I'm focusing on persuasive writing in class.

Examples are given below; pupils should be encouraged to add to these:

Time Running Out

1.   *We need to act now or* ....

2.   *Soon it will be too late to* ....

3.   *We only have limited time so* ....

4.   *Time is running out so* ....

5.   *The clock is ticking* ....

6.   *Time is of the essence because* ....

7.   *The situation is getting worse as we speak* ....

8.   *The situation is a ticking time bomb* ....

LANGUAGE TECHNIQUE ELEVEN
Surreal Similes (fish needs a bicycle)

Examples: *Our school needs junk food like a bald man needs a hairdryer.*
Our school needs junk food like a horse needs a moped.

To create a 'surreal simile' begin by writing a statement which is the exact opposite of your persuasive position. In the two examples above the point of the persuasive essay is that the school DOES NOT need junk food. So we start with "Our school needs ...". The latter part of the sentence begins with 'like a' and concludes with a phrase which conjures a ludicrous image.

To help pupils to write the latter half of the 'surreal simile' I ask them to think of an animal or person e.g. dog/pilot/fish.

Then they have to think of things that their animal or person would never need:

Dog – cat food
Pilot – flying lessons
Fish–bicycle.

These are then added together to produce the 'surreal simile'.

N.B. If the persuasive essay is about a particularly grave / deeply emotional subject then a 'surreal simile' would be inappropriate.

LANGUAGE TECHNIQUE TWELVE

Suppose x 3 .... then a final question.

> Example:
> *__Suppose__ smoking reduced your lifespan by one year?*
> *__Suppose__ smoking reduced your lifespan by five years?*
> *__Suppose__ smoking reduced your lifespan by 10 years?*
> *__How many__ years would you need to lose before you gave up?* OR
> *__Would you__ start if you knew that experts suggest it's more like five years?*

This technique, once again, uses both deliberate repetition and deliberate dramatic heightening (one year, five years etc.).

The word 'suppose' can be replaced by 'imagine'.

Each time the question is asked a possible (negative) future is imagined. Following the three questions with the repeating 'Suppose / imagine' stem, a final question implicitly or explicitly functions as a 'call to action'.

The technique can, of course, be inverted so that the first three questions suggest a positive future which is then explicitly negated by a final statement (rather than question).

> Example:
> *__Can you imagine__ running a marathon at 80?*
> *__Can you imagine__ taking up surfing at the same age?*
> *__Can you imagine__ having a long and happy retirement?*
> *Well, I guarantee you that none of this will happen if you smoke.*

LANGUAGE TECHNIQUE THIRTEEN
End of Sentence Impact

If we structure a sentence so that the final word of that sentence is the word which we wish to emphasise, then the persuasive power of that word is amplified.

> Example: *Smoking can <u>kill</u>. Smoking will <u>kill</u>.*
> *If the road is built you could <u>die</u>.*
> *This can only end in <u>tragedy</u>.*

Note that the final word is usually highly emotive.
(See also Language Technique Three - Yoked Sentences, page 27)

LANGUAGE TECHNIQUE FOURTEEN
Adverbs of manner

An adverb of manner intensifies the emotional impact of a verb –

They will drive dangerously.
   (verb)   (adverb of manner)

It can kill quickly.
(verb) (adverb of manner)

It will ruin completely.
   (verb)   (adverb of manner)

Make an A-Z poster of useful 'ly' words to use in persuasive writing. A photocopiable example is included on the next page. Pupils should be encouraged to add to this so that its production is a cumulative process.

ADVERBS
OF MANNER
An A-Z of 'ly' words for persuasive writing
(Positive and Negative)

A   Atrociously, Awfully, Annoyingly, Alarmingly

B   Brilliantly

C   Cruelly

D   Dangerously

E   Extremely

F   Frighteningly

G   Generously

H   Horribly

I   Irritatingly

J   Jovially

K   Kindly

L   Lovingly

M   Madly

N   Nastily

O   Openly

P   Persuasively, Perilously

Q   Quickly

R   Repeatedly

S   Shockingly, Shamefully

T   Terribly

U   Unhappily

V   Violently

W   Weakly

Z   Zealously

LANGUAGE TECHNIQUE FIFTEEN
We and They

The pronouns 'We' and 'They' are immensely powerful if used correctly (and not over-used!).

The word 'we' should be used sparingly but when used its inclusive nature directly links both the audience and the writer: the persuader and the audience to be persuaded are connected as one unit.

When teaching how to use the pronoun 'we', I model paragraphs which mainly use sentences which begin with the first person pronoun 'I' but always end with a sentence beginning with the plural pronoun 'we'. This makes the key 'persuasive punch' (at the end of the sentence) more powerful. The final 'we' sentence can be a call to action as in the example below.

> *I think that smoking is foolish.*
> *I think that smoking is wrong.*
> *I think that smoking is antisocial.*
> *I know that we all want smoking banned.*

Conversely, the word 'they' excludes; it separates those who support the counter-argument and distances them. The biggest mistake that pupils make with regard to the use of pronouns (in persuasive writing) is the overuse of the word 'they'.

Consider example (A):

> *They say that smoking doesn't harm you. They say that smoking won't kill you. They say that they know people who've lived to 100 and smoked for more than 80 years. We disagree!*

This is an ineffective use of 'They'. It offers three counterarguments and actually lends weight to the pro-smoking faction.

Far better is example (B):

> *They say smoking won't harm you. I say it will harm you. Experts agree with me that it will harm you. Statistics prove that it will severely harm you and I know that we all want it banned.*

In example (B) the pro-smoking counterargument is acknowledged but, importantly, it is not developed and no supporting examples are offered. This is quite correct – a good persuasive essay will acknowledge the opposite viewpoint but it will not give it equal weight with the persuasive point.

If it did, it would actually be an example of a 'Balanced Argument' rather than a persuasive text.

LANGUAGE TECHNIQUE SIXTEEN
Multisensory Language

This was explored in Opener Ten (page 20). It can be used at any stage in a persuasive essay, particularly when anecdotal evidence (with which the writer intends the reader to identify) is introduced.

Useful persuasive sentence starters which appeal to each of the senses:

Taste

I couldn't stomach ....
The idea that X could / couldn't occur is like a poison.
It is a bitter pill to swallow ....
To lose would be like ashes in my mouth.
Do we want to taste defeat?
It turns my stomach ....

Smell

They suggest X but I smell a rat.
They won't come up smelling of roses ....
The heady scent of victory ....
So if you want a fresh breeze to blow through ....

Sound

If we are going to sound the trumpets of victory ....
I wonder if they can hear the slow funeral bell ringing for their argument.
We should become a chorus of disapproval ....

Sight

Their clouded view ....
We can see clearly that the outcome of ....
A useful eye-opener would be ....

Touch

To grasp the importance of ....
So let's seize the opportunity to ....
Let's not allow them to take matters into their own hands.
We will point the way toward the truth.
We must kick their idea into touch.

As is the case with many of the ideas discussed in this book, overuse will make the approach seem hackneyed.

LANGUAGE TECHNIQUE
SEVENTEEN
'CERTAINTY' words and phrases

'CERTAINTY' words and phrases indicate that there is no doubt in the writer's mind. They are often used to start key sentences.

1. *Unquestionably* ....

2. *Without a doubt* ....

3. *No one can argue that* ....

4. *Irrefutably* ....

5. *It is 100% certain that* ....

6. *A known fact* ....

7. *It has been proven that* ....

8. *The undeniable proof is* ....

LANGUAGE TECHNIQUE EIGHTEEN
If ...... then

The 'If....then' combination is a powerful one as it demonstrates how simple it is to achieve an outcome.

I teach pupils that this combination is often most effective before the final 'call to action' as in the two following examples:

> *If you donate only £1 every month, then the suffering of at least three animals would stop. We can do this together. Send £1 now and start making a difference.*

> *If you only do 15 minutes of exercise a day then you could live up to ten years longer. How can you not afford 15 minutes?*

LANGUAGE TECHNIQUE NINETEEN
Puns

Example

The new road. It's something to die for!

A pun is a play on words. The above example plays on the phrase 'something to die for!'. We often use this phrase to suggest that we can't wait any longer, as is the case in 'I'm dying for something to eat'.

Used in the context of the example above, it could imply that we can't wait for the new road to be built, BUT in the context of the following persuasive essay the reader very quickly finds out that the outcome – 'to die' could be taken literally.

The 'pun' is a complex form of language manipulation and it should be used sparingly. Used badly it can detract from a persuasive point.

CLOSING STRATEGIES

A range of ways of opening and ending text forms should be explicitly taught. I made this point several years ago in the book **Improving Story Writing at Key Stages 1 & 2** (Nash Pollock Publishing). Without this explicit modelling and discussion of closing strategies, persuasive essays can 'trail off'. Some effective closing strategies are detailed in this chapter.

CLOSING STRATEGY ONE

Urgent Action Needed

Examples

> **1.** So, to conclude, I have only one question for you ... can you really afford to wait any longer?
>
> **2.** Time is running out. The clock is ticking. We haven't got much longer. Can you really walk away and do nothing?
>
> **3.** If we don't act now it will be too late.

In a sense these are all 'calls to action'. It's just that the action needed will have been detailed in the main body of the persuasive text. Note that this conclusion can take the form of either a question or a statement.

CLOSING STRATEGY TWO

Reiteration of the main persuasive points

This technique affords the writer a splendid opportunity to reinforce key points from the essay. There are, however, three rules:

1. Avoid full sentences.
2. Use different (or slightly altered) vocabulary.
3. Avoid prose layout.

The easiest way to achieve all three of these rules is to model a bullet pointed (or alpha ordered / numeric) last paragraph. An example is included below:

To conclude, the motorway should not be built because:

- Pupils couldn't hear in class.

- Respiration problems would increase.

- We could be hurt or even killed by cars, buses or lorries.

CLOSING STRATEGY THREE

Anecdote which is the exact opposite of the one which opened the persuasive essay

Let's consider how this could work, using the 'Opener One' anecdote (page 11):

Opening Anecdote

John was a friendly, well-liked, loving boy. He was loved by his mum, dad, gran and grandad. He was also loved by all his classmates. One day John forgot to look left and right when he came to the busy road in front of his school. Instead he stepped onto the road and a speeding car hit him. John was killed by that speeding car and every day since he has been missed by everyone who knew him.

This is exactly what <u>could</u> happen <u>if</u> the road is built in front of our Primary School.

MAIN BODY OF PERSUASIVE ESSAY

Closing Anecdote

John is a friendly, well-liked, loving boy. He is loved by his mum, dad, gran and grand-dad. He is also loved by all his classmates. John walks to school without a care in the world and none of his family worries about him. Why? It's because the road has not been built. If you want this happy ending for John and his family then please act now.

Note that in the closing anecdote the past tense sentences are deliberately changed to present tense. Note also that the anecdote is followed by a 'call to action'.

CLOSING STRATEGY FOUR
'Double Bind' Ending

A 'double blind' ending consists of two questions each of which asks if the opposite of the persuasive viewpoint is wanted / accepted. Following these two questions the essay concludes with a categorical statement that neither of the things suggested in the question is wanted – what is wanted is the direct opposite (the point argued for throughout the essay).

Example

Are we a school which wants junk food from (INSERT BRAND NAME 1 HERE) ?

Are we a school which wants junk food from (INSERT BRAND NAME 2 HERE) ?

No, in our school we want healthy food and in this essay we've proved why healthy food is so important for all children.

CONCLUSION

I hope the ideas included in this book have added to your teaching repertoire. Please link them to persuasive writing tasks which relate to pupils' interests and ensure that the range of audiences is as broad as possible.

This approach will ensure that the techniques have maximum impact. Used in this way the features of the text form discussed in this book can form discrete writing targets within the activity.

If we are going to raise writing standards, then pupils need to enjoy the writing process. This should be the first principle which underpins the teaching of any text type!

Alan Peat
2011

SENTENCE STARTERS
(...which support the persuasive viewpoint)

1. A compelling reason...

2. Additionally...

3. As you can see...

4. Certainly...

5. Don't forget that...

6. Furthermore...

7. I'd also like to draw your attention to...

8. Importantly...

9. Last but by no means least...

10. Moreover...

11. Obviously...

12. Of overwhelming importance...

13. Of paramount importance...

14. One clear reason...

15. Still not convinced? Please read on...

16. The most powerful reason for thinking/supporting...

17. There is no doubt...

18. Undeniably...

19. Unquestionably...

20. Without a doubt...

SENTENCE STARTERS
(...which demolish the opposing viewpoint)

1. A compelling reason why we should not...

2. Although, at first glance (opposing point) seems sensible, in reality it...

3. As all intelligent people agree...

4. Do not...

5. Don't accept...

6. Don't trust...

7. If you really want 'peace of mind', then don't...

8. It cannot be said/claimed that...

9. Nobody can sensibly suggest that...

10. Oddly...

11. One overwhelming reason why we shouldn't...

12. One staggering reason not...

13. Other people wrongly suggest... but...

14. Others, with less experience, suggest that...

15. Shockingly...

16. Staggeringly...

17. The argument for (opposing point) is inadequate because...

18. The argument for (opposing point) is questionable because...

19. They would have you believe that...

20. Unbelievably...

SENTENCE STARTERS
(...which conclude the persuasive essay)

1. As you can see...

2. Can you really afford not to...

3. Don't forget:

4. Finally...

5. I know you'll agree...

6. I'm sure you will now agree that...

7. If you are still unsure, then let me remind you...

8. In conclusion...

9. In conclusion, don't accept...

10. Remember,

11. So, don't be fooled by...

12. So, if you care deeply about...

13. The only intelligent response...

14. The only logical conclusion is...

15. There's only one answer...

16. To conclude, don't be taken in by...

17. To conclude, I urge you to...

18. To sum up...

19. To summarise...

20. You have the right to demand...

PERSUASIVE
QUESTION STEMS

1. Are you confused by...?

2. Are you ready to...?

3. Are you still...?

4. Ask yourself...?

5. Can you believe that...?

6. Did you know that...?

7. Do they realise that...?

8. Do we want...?

9. Don't we need...?

10. Have we time to...?

11. Have you considered...?

12. How can they...?

13. How do they...?

14. How many times...?

15. How would you feel if...?

16. Isn't it time we...?

17. What cost...?

18. What would you say if...?

19. Why accept...?

20. Wouldn't you prefer to...?

have negative impact
beyond the bounds of decency
regretful
substandard
inferior
awful
have dire consequences
create panic
lose-lose situation

unfit
erroneous
high-risk
immoral
risky
serious objections
terrible
raise serious objections
will 'end in tears'
made the situation worse

lacking in thought
worsen the situation
unsound
dreadful
appalling
harmful
have serious consequences
impact negatively
hurt
have negative consequences evil

amazing

marvellous

worthy

astonishing
favourable

sensational

solid

smashing

honest

right

effective

impact positively

advantageous

absolutely fantastic

just

safe

incomparable

unforgettable

utterly fabulous

virtuous

acceptable

great

sound

honourable

positive impact

undreamt of

tremendous

beneficial

satisfactory

splendid

incredible

moral

striking

superb

salutary

unparalleled

MAKE YOUR POINT!

WHAT I THINK

TIPS
Start with I.
Don't use 'good' or 'bad'.
Use a double bind:
"Are we a school which ...
Are we a school which ..."

WHY I THINK IT 1

TIPS
Start with your strongest argument
Ask a question of the reader:
"How would you feel if.."
Use dramatic heightening:
"Hurt ... maimed ... killed".

WHY I THINK IT 2

TIPS
Use numbers/percentages/graphs.

WHY I THINK IT 3

TIPS
"Another reason ..."
Use certainty phrases:
"Undoubtedly..."
"It is certain that ..."

WHAT OTHERS THINK

TIPS
Use one or two opposing arguments, then "...however."

WHY I STILL THINK IT

TIPS
Use three reasons given below,
using different language.
"To sum up, I still think ...'
because
• (use bullet points) OR
1. (numbers) OR
A. (letters)

EXPAND YOUR POINT!

MAKE YOUR POINT AGAIN!

EXAMPLE
OF PUPIL'S WORK

SCHOOL: Wyche Primary School, Worcestershire
TEACHER: Jon Westwood
PUPIL: Milly Jackson-Read, age 11

Simply The Best

Do you know someone who was so ill they had no chance of surviving? Do you know someone who strived to survive? Do you know someone who almost died? I do. Her name is Maria Starr.

At the age of nine Maria caught cancer and was fighting against it for two whole years. On the edge of dying she survived and was brave and jolly the whole time. Always the optimist even at the hardest of time, she was never down!

Maria is truly special and fortunate that she is still here today. Maria prays for those who unlike her did not make it.

What Maria has done is heroic and that makes her an idol, an idol to those like her. Maria is outstanding and now every year does the race for life to help others that are in her position.

Overall Maria is truly a 'star' (and that's not just because of her surname!). Maria Starr is honestly and truly special! Can you think of anyone better for the 'simply the best' award?

EXAMPLE
OF PUPIL'S WORK

SCHOOL: Wyche Primary School, Worcestershire
TEACHER: Jon Westwood
PUPIL: Rhys Leonard, age 11

Worried about value for money? You should be. You are being ripped off by expensive packs with rubbish contents.

For six pounds, in an average pack you get a small number of cards, a cheap rubber toy and maybe, if you're lucky, a pencil. What a rip-off! However, the World cup 2010 pack IS value for money, with over five toys and a chance to win a signed England shirt, for an amazing offer of £5.50! Your child will love it. The toys are strong and durable with a five-year guarantee.

Joe Williamson, a local newspaper agent worker shares his opinion:

"I've run this shop for five years now and 60% of people who come here buy some of these rip-off packs that usually break before you get home. But this World Cup pack is DEFINITELY value for money and is hard and durable."

Others think that this is just another of those freebie packs and is rubbish like all those average packs. However, you haven't seen the World Cup 2010 pack. The quality items within the pack will change minds and opinions. Produced by happy workers in a reliable and recognised factory, the World Cup pack is guaranteed quality.

You should buy the World Cup pack because:

- It is value for money
- It has quality items
- It guarantees fun for your child.

EXAMPLE
OF PUPIL'S WORK

SCHOOL: Wyche Primary School, Worcestershire
TEACHER: Jon Westwood
PUPIL: Amelia Trevelyan, age 11

Bob was happy. His mum had bought him a magazine called Football Mad! But when Bob got home, he found his free toys broken. The magazine was long and boring. Bob was heart-broken. Don't let your children be heart-broken. Buy the World Cup 2010 Football Pack. It is value for money.

In your World Cup Football Pack, you get five raffle tickets to win a genuine England shirt, signed by the England team. Is that value for money or what?

Apart from your raffle tickets, you also get in your pack a drinks bottle with the flags of all the countries taking part in the World Cup on it.

Generously, we also put in a coaching whistle, a World Cup ruler, pencil and much more. WOW! That's value for money!

Rob Lever, a local newsagent, said: "After seeing the World Cup football pack, I've realised that 75% of other packs are NOT value for money!" Shamefully, Rob Lever is right!

Frighteningly, you pay £6 for one Pokemon pack! Scarily, you pay £5.50 for cartoon magazines! Atrociously you get ripped off five times a day! That's a fact!

However there are other mothers who don't believe that this pack is value for money. But they don't know about the signed England shirt, the water bottle, the ruler and other goodies! They would rather buy that £6 Pokemon pack! Now that really is "value for money"?

Bob isn't broken-hearted now. He enjoys coaching his friends with his whistle, he proudly wears his England shirt that he won and he jovially quenches his thirst with his water bottle. All because his mum bought the World Cup 2010 Football Pack! Don't make the same mistake as Bob's mother. Buy the World Cup 2010 Football Pack. It is value for money!

EXAMPLE
OF PUPIL'S WORK

SCHOOL: Castle View Primary, Halton
TEACHER: Rachel Jones
PUPIL: Chloe Davies, age 11

Stop the deadly incinerator!

Lily was a beautiful young four-year-old playing in the park with her friends where she spent most of her day. Beautiful little Lily loved making daisy chains. She used to take her doll and pram with her to the park. Lily used to ride high on the red and rusty swings. Going down the slide she squealed! But one horrible misty day, little Lily got cancer. She never went back to the park again. She never saw her friends again. This could happen if the awful incinerator is built.

Firstly, the deadly incinerator will give off an atrocious dioxin and this awful gas can cause cancer.

The second reason is that a lot of this monstrous dioxin will be put into Runcorn's air. Most of the pollution will go into the water underground.

Furthermore, when it rains, it washes all of the pollutants into rivers and streams and into our tap water. It will affect us when we drink and it might go into our showers and baths. It won't be very healthy. Dr Jones told me that the cancer rates would go up by 21%. He does not want this horrible incinerator to be built.

Another reason is that the traffic will be building up in Runcorn. All of the rubbish is coming from Warrington, Runcorn, Widnes, Cheshire, Manchester, Halton and Liverpool – basically the whole of the North West! Massive, monstrous large lorries, just imagine the trash dropping out of these lorries. The whole of the North-West will be covered in trash. It won't be very nice!

On the other hand, other people think that it will be good to have the incinerator so rubbish will not be buried under the ground. However, nothing will be recycled and when there is no paper left, children at school will have nothing to write on.

Do you want people to die? I don't! Tell the community that the incinerator should not be built; it is too much of a disaster. Stop it. We don't want our children to get cancer do we?

EXAMPLE
OF PUPIL'S WORK

SCHOOL: Wyche Primary School, Worcestershire
TEACHER: Jon Westwood
PUPIL: Abigail Oldroyd

Fox Hunting: Banned Or Not?

The issue being discussed is whether fox hunting should be banned or not.

Some think that fox hunting is a fun sport; others think that it is cruel and unnecessary.

People say that foxes have as many rights as we do to live. If we don't kill them for food, why kill them at all? However, the dog owners claim that the dogs are highly trained and only kill the weak and ill foxes. The dogs are saving the fox from a painful death by putting it out of its misery so it doesn't have to suffer.

There are many people who have concerns about the number of foxes in Britain. Like in other countries, animals are hunted to extinction. But the hunters claim that they only kill one in ten foxes so there's nothing to worry about!

The chase, as many people protest, is an agonizing, hectic and startling death. It has been proven by scientists that the dogs rip the fox from limb to limb. The dogs only get exercise from the chase; they never really get anything else. It is very rare that a fox is caught because the healthy fox is too fast compared to the dog.

As you can see both sides have many opinions but I personally think that fox hunting should stay banned because foxes have as much right to live as we do to stay alive.

EXAMPLE
OF PUPIL'S WORK

SCHOOL: Castle View Primary, Halton
TEACHER: Rachel Jones
PUPIL: Lucie Webb, age 11

Should P.E. be stopped in schools?

Joel is eight years old and he loves PE. He loves competing against others in bench ball, dodge ball, football and lots of other different sports. Also, in dodge ball, he is always the last one standing; he never gives up in any kind of sport. His team always wins in bench ball and everyone loves him in sports! Everyone says that he is fantastic and amazing, he always cheers people on even if they think they are not good at a game. This could all change if P.E. is taken off the timetable and it will be a disaster.

Firstly, all of the children will give up trying to be sporty and they will be becoming slower and slower whenever they have to get a pencil or a ruler. Even though they have play-time, they will stop running around, because they are getting more tired by the minute.

Furthermore, childrens' doctors have been saying (angrily):

"These children have not got enough exercise! 87% of children in this area are becoming fatter, just because they don't have P.E. in school! This is despicable!"

Joel doesn't like going to school any more, instead he wants to stay at home because there is no more P.E. in school. In addition, he is getting later each day for school because he can't walk very fast. He is trying to get to school on time, but it is too hard for him.

Many people say that English, maths and science are much more important to children and they need a good education. However, if children want to be in the Olympics when they are older, they need plenty of exercise. Also the brain will get slower and they won't be as quick to answer questions in lessons.

The evidence is clear that children need P.E. and lots of exercise. Joel is very unhappy now because he can't answer any questions and people keep bullying him. Would you want to destroy Joel's chance to be an athlete in the future? In the future everyone will be happier if P.E. is on the timetable.

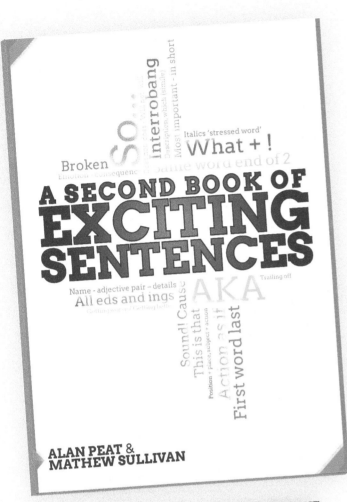
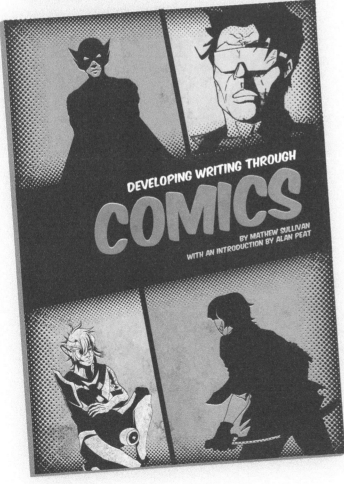

50 Ways to Retell a Story:
Cinderella
by Alan Peat, Julie Peat
& Christopher Storey

Get Your Head Around
Punctuation
(and how to teach it)
by Alan Peat

Writing Exciting Sentences
Age 7 Plus
by Alan Peat

Improving Non-fiction Writing
at Key Stage 1 & 2:
The Success Approach
by Margaret McNeil
& Alan Peat

Improving Story Writing
at Key Stage 1 & 2
by Alan Peat

Word Games
at Key Stage 2
by Alan Peat

Teaching Poetry
with 7 - 12 year olds
by Alan Peat

Teaching Poetry
with 4 - 8 year olds
by Alan Peat

Buy
more of
Alan Peat's
books from
www.thecepress.com